Praise for *Mindfulness. In the Maelstrom of Life*

"I bow to Edel Maex for writing this lovely book, and [illegible] relentless efforts to bring mindfulness in an authentic and universal articulation, based on his own years of meditation practice and study, into the mainstream of medicine, psychiatry, and Western culture." – *Jon Kabat-Zinn, Professor of Medicine emeritus, University of Massachusetts Medical School*

"Dr. Edel Maex has written a heartfelt, wonderfully nuanced primer on mindfulness that supports it nurturing and steady movement into our daily lives. I highly recommend it." – *Zindel V. Segal, Distinguished Professor of Psychology in Mood Disorders, University of Toronto Scarborough*

"What a delight! This book is like a peaceful conversation, rich and dense. The mix of personal meditation experience, his professional experience as a psychotherapist, counselling techniques and zen wisdom transforms reading this book into an immediate mindfulness exercise: while reading, you take the time to pause and reflect. The journey has already begun…." – *Christophe André, psychiatrist at the Saint-Anne Hospital in Paris*

"This book invites the reader to make an appointment with himself, in an open and welcoming spirit. It seems so simple. In reality, this requires, as any other form of training, the daily discipline to perform mindful exercises and meditations. Edel Maex gives us different keys to sit, to maintain and to develop our mindfulness practice, with an exceptional clarity and a lot of wisdom. An admirably clear, didactic book. I would recommend it to all participants of our MBCT-courses and their instructors." – *Lucio Bizzini, Ph.D, Department of Psychiatry, University Hospital of Geneva*

MIND
FUL
NESS

Edel Maex

MIND
In the maelstrom
FUL
of life
NESS

LANNOO

CONTENTS

4 Practicing with what is there

5 A continuous process of healing

6 To create a space of kind, open attention…

7 Getting comfortable with not knowing

8 The eighth week lasts the rest of your life

THANKS

Inexpressible thanks go out to a number of people, without whom this book could never have come into being. In the first place to Thich Nhat Hanh, Zen teacher, peace activist, exile, and poet. He is the one who, in the terror of the Vietnam War, plucked the term mindfulness from the broad assortment of Buddhist concepts as the quintessential point of entry. He was present as mindfulness flowered in the West.

My thanks also go out to Jon Kabat-Zinn, who, building on the work of Thich Nhat Hanh and various other Zen and Vipassana teachers, drew mindfulness from its Buddhist context and introduced it to the world of medicine and science through his eight-week stress reduction course.

But most of all I would like to thank the hundreds of people who followed the eight-week program and who surprised me time and time again (and continue to surprise me) with the way in which they recognize mindfulness and give it a place in the maelstrom of their lives.

FOREWORD

by Jon Kabat-Zinn

If you are like most people, you are probably working harder, juggling more tasks, and feeling like you have less and less time for what is important in life than ever before. In a word, you have never felt more stressed. Today, I think back to 1979, when I started the mindfulness-based stress reduction (MBSR) clinic at the University of Massachusetts Medical Center, and ask I myself: "1979? What stress?" The pace of life and the demands on our time and energy have greatly increased over the past few decades, partly due to the digital revolution and the speeding up of just about everything, partly due to other factors that make it hard for us as human beings to live lives of balance and clarity, no matter what the circumstances.

It is a fact that today, for many of us, the workday or the workweek seem to have no end. We no longer even need a workplace, as anyplace can become a workplace by virtue of our 24/7 connectivity. The digital revolution has its advantages of course, but these can be extremely seductive, even addictive. With all the *other*-connectivity, as well as the infinite ways in which we can distract ourselves from the matter at hand, we may be drifting further and further from any meaningful and embodied connection to ourselves and those we love the most. Perhaps we need to take extra precautions to purposefully and tenaciously nurture those fundamental human connections — both the inner and the outer ones — that most characterize our humanity and sense of well-being and purpose. Part of this nurturance involves a shift from doing to being, at least in certain moments. Part of it involves recognizing that we only have moments to live, in the sense that we are only alive now, in this moment, and that the present moment is easily missed or even evaded if it is unpleasant or threatening. We may be more asleep than awake in our lives, moving along on auto-pilot most of the time, and as a consequence, drift ever further out of touch with our deepest loves and yearnings, and from our deep inner and innate resources for learning and growing, as well as for healing and transformation across our life span.

This condition can be remedied in large measure through the intentional cultivation of mindfulness, or moment to moment non-judgmental awareness. In this lovely and very user-friendly book, Dr. Edel Maex gives us an excellent introduction to this cultivation and to the potential transformations of mind and body, heart and soul, that are available to us in every moment if we can, as he describes it, stop and then look and listen deeply before we act. I encourage the reader to listen attentively to his deceptively simple yet powerful messages and to practice wholeheartedly what he is offering us so eloquently and gently in these pages.

There is a growing body of scientific and medical evidence that the cultivation of mindfulness can make a profound difference to one's mental and physical health, positively affecting the body's capacity for healing, the brain's capacity for continually fine-tuning itself and growing new pathways, and the ability of the heart and mind to wisely handle stress, pain, illness, and above all, suffering, in ways that are both liberating and transformative. Indeed, there is a growing movement in both medicine and psychology throughout the world to develop mindfulness-based clinical programs, such as the program offered by Edel Maex and his colleagues, and to conduct both basic and applied research on the effects of mindfulness on the mind and body, and on social and emotional interaction and learning.

There is also poetry to living in the present moment, expressed in words beyond words, pointing to the transcendent and the numinous in every moment, not in some dogmatic religious way, but in a more universal, humanistic gesture that lies at the foundation of all great works of art and their appreciation. One could say, as Thoreau did, that a human life that is lived in awareness, fully awake, is the greatest of arts. In this book, you will encounter poetic indicators of where the cultivation of mindfulness might carry us. And it always carries us back to the here and now. You will find that Dr. Maex appreciates the songs of Leonard Cohen, himself a life-long practitioner of mindfulness in the Zen tradition. So here are some lines from Leonard Cohen to whet your appetite and prepare your palate for what is yet to come.

The birds they sang
At the break of day.
Start again, I heard them say.
Don't dwell on what is passed away,
Or what is yet to come.
Ring the bell that still can ring
Forget your perfect offering.
There is a crack, a crack in everything,
That's how the light gets in,
That's how the light gets in,
That's how the light gets in....

The convergence of the streams of science and medicine with the streams of art and poetry, both flowing into and exploring the ancient currents of meditation practice in our modern era make the present moment a very exciting time to explore the cultivation of mindfulness in one's own life. This cultivation is, in and of itself, an act of wisdom and of self-compassion, as you will no doubt discover for yourself through paying attention as described within these pages. Learning to rest in and trust awareness itself, without having to make anything happen to improve on the present moment. That is the great invitation and also the great life adventure that is being extended to you here. May it be of profound benefit to your own life, and also to the many other beings with whom you come in contact and with whom you share your life.

I bow to Edel Maex for writing this lovely book, and for his relentless efforts to bring mindfulness in an authentic and universal articulation, based on his own years of meditation practice and study, into the mainstream of medicine, psychiatry, and Western culture.

Jon Kabat-Zinn, Ph.D.
Professor of Medicine emeritus
University of Massachusetts Medical School

0

NO ONE HAS EVER LEARNED TO PLAY THE PIANO BY READING A BOOK

BACKGROUND

A long time ago, while I was finishing my education as a psychiatrist, I came face to face with one big question: How can I survive the daily confrontation with so much human pain, sorrow, anxiety, trauma, and loss? I had to find a way to sail safely between two dangerous rocks. On the one hand, there was the risk I would be overwhelmed by all the pain and emotion and suffer a burnout myself. On the other hand, I was in danger of shutting out my own feelings and becoming emotionless, objective, unavailable, untouched by my patients' pain.

As I was searching for an answer, one thing led to another, and I found out about Zen meditation. This was the answer to my question. Clearly, meditation was "my thing." I have learned an awful lot from it. Not only has it shaped my work, it also has had a big impact on how I live my daily life.

Some ten years after I started practicing meditation, I began thinking: "This is not fair. I'm keeping the best for myself." The problem was that I had no idea how to present Zen meditation to my patients within a psychotherapeutic context. I couldn't just start practicing Buddhist meditation in a hospital! And how could I explain to someone seeking relief from their pain that they had to sit in silence for a half hour and not expect anything at all from it? The Zen method is not very accessible for those unfamiliar with it.

I began experimenting by weaving into my work some elements of meditation. Then one day someone asked me, "Don't you know about the work of Jon Kabat-Zinn?" I had never heard of him, but quickly went out and found the book—still unread—in the library of the Helen Dowling Institute where I was working at the time. I realized immediately, "This will save me ten years of work!" Jon Kabat-Zinn had a similar background to mine and with similar aspirations he had created a stress-reduction program. This program was being conducted in a hospital and was the subject of thorough scientific research which showed it to be an acceptable tool in the medical world. I realized that I did not have to invent the wheel. I got in touch with Jon Kabat-Zinn and began an eight-week training program based on his work. Many more would follow.

Since then I have trained thousands of people. The context of my training programs has varied considerably. Participants included people with serious illnesses like cancer; people in the helping professions, volunteers in palliative care programs; people with recurring depressions and anxiety attacks; people who suffer chronic fatigue; people with symptoms due to constant stress; employees of various companies.... No matter what the context is, all participants are confronted with the same fundamental issues.

This book contains the heart of all these meetings. I am writing it with the hope of sharing the best of what I know without holding anything back.

BOOK LEARNING

No one has ever learned how to play the piano by reading a book. You learn how to play a musical instrument by by playing it again and again and again. There is no single book, theory, or teacher that can take the place of practice and your own experience. This is equally true for mindfulness.

So what is the purpose of this book? You can read it as an introduction. A book can help you to get acquainted with something. This book is not meant to give you a lot of theory or scientific facts — there are already lots of fine theoretical books on the market. What I want is to give you a taste of mindfulness and inspire you to actually begin practicing it. Even though I want to share with you the best that I have learned, I know that this is not something I can teach you. You can only learn mindfulness by doing it yourself. Maybe this book will inspire you to follow an eight-week mindfulness training. Then it will serve as an excellent support throughout your practice, as it presents the training and the themes that come up naturally during the eight weeks. You can look at it as being composed of eight movements. Some themes reoccur regularly and are expanded and deepened as we go on. As you go along, this book will give you practical suggestions about dealing with the circumstances of your daily life and offer insights into some difficult situations and traps.

Remember that no one has a monopoly on mindfulness. The eight-week program is simply a compact and intense presentation of something that is at least 2,500 years old. Even if you are practicing other methods of mindfulness, this book may offer you support as well as useful and practical tips.

STRESS IS UNAVOIDABLE

Sometimes life resembles a river that flows along its bed without any disturbance. Then suddenly things can take an unexpected turn and change into a raging maelstrom. It is at that point that life asks the best from us.

Stress is a general term. It stands for everything that can bother us. We can get sick; worry about relationships, work, money. At times we can be asked too much and become exhausted. The things that seemed certain and secure for us today can turn into a big question mark tomorrow. Sometimes life just no longer seems to go the way we want it and nobody can tell us what has gone wrong. Stress can creep into our lives quietly and unrecognized, or it can hit us like a flash of lightning out of the clear sky, turning our lives upside down. Most of the time stress creeps up on us unexpectedly, without our asking for it.

There are two sides to stress: the things that happen to us and how our organism reacts to them.

Our body is our only stress detector. It is with good reason that we call "feelings" feelings. We feel with our body. The body is the only instrument we have which can feel. A computer does not have feelings because it has no body. This is why stress can cause bodily symptoms.

There is a third factor in this equation: How do we deal with stress? We cannot control the things that happen to us and the automatic reactions of our body. We can however influence how we respond to these reactions. Here, we have a choice.

Research shows that the effects of stress are determined by how we respond to it. Mindfulness is a unique way to respond to what happens to us. This is true not just for stress but also for the pleasurable things that happen to us. But it is precisely stress and suffering that most often motivate us to go searching and to learn more about mindfulness.

TRAINING

What do we practice in mindfulness training? In the very first exercise you are invited to lie down on a mat and to become aware of your breathing. However, unlike other methods, you are not asked to change anything about your breathing—you do not have to try abdominal breathing, you do not have to breathe deeper or more smoothly. You are simply asked to pay attention to your breathing without any judgment, in a kind and open way (this is a definition of mindfulness). You continue by becoming aware of the toes on your left foot and then, step by step, you will become aware of your whole body. Without any further suggestions, without asking to relax. Just become aware of what is going on, with kind openness.

What is the point of doing this?

First of all, focusing on your breathing interrupts what you usually do. Many problems arising from stress stem from the fact that we just keep going on and on. We feel like we lose control and we are drawn into the maelstrom of life.

Furthermore, this exercise enables you to start getting acquainted with what is going on inside of you. We deliberately chose a physical approach, as the body is the only stress detector we have. Most of the time we only begin to take notice of our body when it is too late, when we begin to experience symptoms. By focusing on our breathing, we can learn to feel what is happening inside us before the symptoms set in. Obviously, we cannot respond to something we are not aware of or have no idea that it even exists. It could be that, by focusing on your breathing, you develop your ability to relax. Most likely you will become aware of tension. This is important, even though at first it is probably not very pleasant. Needless to say, all kinds of feelings and thoughts come up during this exercise. The exercises that follow look more deeply into how we can respond to these thoughts and feelings.

Finally, mindfulness itself is another way of responding to what happens to us. It is the middle path between two rocks. On one side is the danger of consciously or unconsciously denying what you are feeling; on the other is the risk of being caught up in what is going on and be dragged along. This is one of the reasons why practice is so important. You learn how to feel and to maintain contact with your feelings while at the same time you avoid being mastered by those feelings. One aspects of mindfulness training is to constantly bring yourself back to the middle way.

EIGHT WEEKS

The eight-week-long mindfulness training is based on the work of Jon Kabat-Zinn. It is certainly not the only way to learn mindfulness, but I find it a very instructive method.

We call it training and not a treatment or a course. A treatment would imply something that you passively submit to for eight weeks hoping that at the end, the problem will be solved. This is not the case. It is also not a course, even though there are some elements of insight involved. To know what can go wrong and what to do about it is certainly important, but it is not enough. Mindfulness is a form of training. We are going to practice something.

The training consists of two-and-a-half-hour weekly sessions, eight weeks in a row. Participants make a commitment to practicing for 45 minutes each day. It may not be immediately obvious, but participating without practicing would be the same as taking piano lessons without doing your homework every day. Our experience has shown that 45 minutes practice each day for eight weeks is enough to learn what the basics of mindfulness are about without it becoming burdensome. You can look at it as an experiment with yourself. Suspend your judgment for this period and allow yourself to fully taste your experience. At the end of the eight weeks, you can see what you have learned from the experiment and decide if and how you want to continue further.

During the training, various practices will be introduced to you. There are "formal" practices, such as sitting meditation and simple physical exercises. There are also various "informal" practices, things you can pay attention to in your daily life, for example when you are eating or when you are stuck in a traffic jam. You also receive homework assignments, such as observing what happens to you during pleasant or unpleasant experiences.

During the first two weeks, we focus on the body scan. This is an exercise whereby you lie down and systematically become aware of each part of your body. This can be deeply relaxing and bring you into closer contact with your body.

In the next two weeks we work more actively with the body. The body scan is alternated with simple stretching exercises. These teach you to become aware of the sensations in your body when you reach your limits. You learn to feel your boundaries without going beyond them. You also learn not to stop too early and possibly will expand your movement potential.

Throughout these first four weeks, the practice of sitting meditation is gradually introduced. The emphasis is on becoming calm as well as being aware of what is going on inside and around you. Alongside working with your body, you begin to pay attention to your feelings and to communication with others. Homework assignments help you to pause and look at small events in your daily life, and to observe how you react to them.

The last sessions explore how you can incorporate the formal and the informal techniques into your daily life.

At the end of the eight weeks, you are free to choose what works best for you. It may be sitting meditation or one of the physical exercises. Maybe you will want to emphasize the informal practices, or maybe the physical exercises work best for you at first and after a while you notice that the sitting meditation feels more appropriate. One of the participants summarized his eight-week training like this: "I see that I am at the beginning of my journey—but now I have a suitcase with me."

START FOR YOURSELF

If you like you can start for yourself right now. Here are some practical tips for those who want to practice by themselves.

1 Practice every day. The exercises are shorter than those in the eight-week program. This makes it easier to keep practicing them long-term. Try to practice daily, even if you only have a couple of minutes. The exercises are not more than instructions. Once you get accustomed to them, you may choose to do the exercises without the spoken instructions.

2 Start with your body. Mindfulness asks us to remain firmly grounded. This is why we start our training by focussing on the body with the body scan exercise. While doing other exercises, try to remain in contact with your bodily experience. Following your breathing is one way to facilitate this.

3 Do not read (or re-read) more than one chapter of this book per day. Let the text sink in. The more your practice, the more meaningful and deeper the text becomes.

4 Stop what you are doing several times a day. Give yourself some moments of conscious breathing.

5 Keep observing yourself and your spontaneous reactions to what happens to you during the day. This way you not only get a better insight in how you react during the formal practices but also how you react throughout your daily activities. Hence, what you learn during the formal practice will gradually begin to affect the rest of your life.

6 Cultivate attention for what is happening around you, the space you are in, the sensations you are having....

7 Be kind to yourself. Kindness, dignity, and respect are words that I will repeat over and over again in this book. They are integral to mindfulness. Without kindness, there is no mindfulness.

SONG 6

I cannot collect stamps
I cannot collect girlie pictures
I cannot accumulate love affairs
or wisdom
I cannot do anything anymore
    I cannot do anything anymore

Why don't I turn off the light
    and don't I go to bed
I want to attempt
    to be naked
    nude who knows frozen purple and pallor
Isn't the all-beginning beginning that way
I don't want to know anything
I don't want to ask
    why
    I didn't become a stamp collector
I will begin to give away my debacle
I will begin to give away my bankruptcy
I will confer myself a piece of poor soil torn to shreds
        trampled soil
        badlands
        an occupied city
I want to be nude
    and begin

Paul Van Ostaijen, 1896-1928

(from *Feasts of Fear and Agony*, New Directions: 1976,
translated by Hidde Van Ameyden van Duym)

1

EVERY INSTANT IS A NEW BEGINNING

BEGINNING

Starting something new is a special moment. You are open-minded and receptive. You do not know what is going to happen. You are open to every possibility.

Mindfulness carries within itself the attitude of the beginner. Open-minded, receptive, ready for anything. Every instant is a new beginning.

It really is so: this instant is new. It has never happened before and it will never happen again. If we could only be aware of this at every moment, then the rest would unfold naturally.

Let us start with the first exercise. Are you able to look at this moment right now with the eyes of a beginner? Where are you? What is this space you are in?

Maybe you are in a place well known to you. Just for this moment let go of that familiarity. Look around you as if you have never been in this place before. It is new. Look around. What do you see? What do you hear? How does the space you are in feel? How does it smell?

Notice how you are sitting. Are you comfortable? Most likely you are holding a book. How does the book feel in your hands? Does it feel heavy or light? What is the texture of the paper, the cover? What color is the paper? The letters? What does the font look like? Does the book smell new or musty?

Take a moment to think about how this book has come into your hands. Maybe you bought it, maybe it was a present, or maybe you borrowed it. Somebody must have written it. Somebody printed it. A lot of work by a lot of people has gone into producing it. Who made the paper? Where did the trees grow? Where do the ink colors come from?

Without sun and rain, the trees could not have grown. The author only knows what he knows because he has learned it from others; because he has gotten feedback from those he has taught. Everything that has gone into this book has no beginning and no end.

What is it like for you to be present in this moment with this kind of awareness?

SEEKING AND FINDING

Some people are skeptical when they start their mindfulness training. They want to give it a chance but do not really believe in it. Others start with the feeling that at last they have found what they have been looking for.

At the beginning, the skeptical attitude is actually the best.

Halfway through the training program, someone said to me: "I'm afraid that again I'm not going to find what I have been looking for." The answer I gave was quick and simple: "That's for sure."

When we go searching for something, we already have in mind some idea of what it is that we are searching for. So we compare everything we find on our journey with that idea and toss it away if it does not fit. It is a process of selection and exclusion. This is a great strategy for finding something that you have lost. But it does not work if you want to discover something new. It certainly is not the right way to practice mindfulness.

The best way to begin mindfulness training is to have an open but critical attitude. You have no idea what you are going to find. You do not select and judge right away. You do your research carefully. You do not look for something in particular, but rather allow yourself to discover.

When you walk through the woods looking for a certain kind of mushroom you wind up seeing only what looks like a mushroom. When you walk through the woods without a specific goal, all the beauty around you surprises you again and again. It is not about succeeding or failing. There is no planned goal that you have to reach. The only thing there is is an open awareness.

I often hear people say: "I would really like to have more self-confidence." How do you develop self-confidence? Confidence is not something you can force. Don't you get suspicious when someone says: "You must have confidence in me"?

Being present in this moment with a kind and open attention, looking without seeking anything in particular, is the best way to become familiar with what is happening around you and inside you. It is the only way to develop confidence and self-confidence.

RELAXATION

"YOU TAME A WILD HORSE TO RIDE IT – NOT TO PUT IT OUT TO PASTURE."

TENKEI ROSHI

Mindfulness training is not a method of relaxation. Just like relaxation, mindfulness training has its origins in the East. At the same time, mindfulness points to a common human phenomenon that can be applied in many different situations.

The comparison with taming a wild horse clearly shows the difference between relaxation and mindfulness training. There is nothing wrong with relaxation. It is very important to withdraw ourselves at times from the busyness of life. The archer's bow cannot always be drawn taut.

But when you feel sad or happy, when you are furious or hopelessly in love, when your house is on fire or you have just won the lottery, then relaxation is not the thing. If we would completely relax during such moments, we would run the risk of missing the intensity of what it is to be alive. There are times when the archer's bow should be drawn taut.

Mindfulness is exactly what we need at such moments. Precisely at moments like these we need more than ever to be present with a receptive attitude, a mild and alert awareness so we can decide to act or not to act, we can enjoy or we can suffer.

Mindfulness is something that needs to be trained. Ideally you do not begin your training when your house is already on fire—just as you should not start sewing your parachute when you sit in front of the open airplane door. Mindfulness is something you need to practice every day, both on days that feel good and days that feel bad.

Mindfulness training is only possible with real kindness and (self) respect. You can only train a horse if you love horses. You have to understand the horse, get a feel for it. With mindfulness training you befriend yourself and get a feel for your own reactions, even in situations that are loaded with tension and stress.

OPEN

Mindfulness does not really mean what it should mean according to the dictionary. It is a concept that breaks through what tries to limit it. It can best be defined as kind, open attention.

Each word is important here. At times mindfulness is simply translated as "paying attention." People then call it "attention-training." However, the word attention has a wrong feel to it. It is like a high school teacher screaming: "Don't look out the window!". Mindfulness is something entirely different. It is much kinder than that.

How does our attention work? If I find something attractive, it draws my attention. I would notice a beautiful woman walking down the street, while the old man I saw ten seconds earlier walked by unnoticed. Things that are threatening or unpleasant also draw our attention. We tend to give as little attention as possible to what we experience as unpleasant; yet at the same time we can get so deeply caught up in unpleasant feelings that we cannot stop paying attention to them. The harder we fight them, the stronger they seem to get.

Mindfulness is open attention. This means that we pay the same attention to the beautiful woman as to the old man, that we pay equal attention to pleasant and unpleasant feelings and thoughts.

Mindfulness is kind attention. The one is not possible without the other. It is impossible to be attentive to everything that presents itself without a big dose of kindness. In order to be honest with yourself, you need to be open to everything. And everything is not always pretty. I sometimes sit on my meditation cushion in the evening and suddenly realize that a couple of hours before I made a stupid mistake, a truly ridiculous blunder... I was so busy during the day that I completely forgot about it. Then I remember it on my cushion and there is no escape. It would be cruel not to be kind to myself when I realize my mistakes. An open, receptive attention is only possible and bearable if we combine it with kindness.

BODY SCAN
ATTENTION AND RELAXATION

Attention is one of our most basic needs. Attention is not only nourishing for our mind, but for our bodies too. However, giving attention to our bodies from the inside out is not an obvious thing to do, especially when we feel pain or discomfort. Then we spontaneously tend to ignore the parts of our body that need attention most.

In the body scan we consciously pay attention to every part of our body. Nourishing attention is kind and non-judgmental. Breathe to every part of your body, especially where it does not feel good. Breathe to the parts where you feel relaxed and fine as well. Sometimes discomfort distracts us from what feels fine.

The body scan can be really relaxing, but avoid *trying* to relax. Relaxation is not something you can consciously control. The more you try to relax, the more tense you might feel. It is like trying to flatten out sea waves or push sand back to the riverbed in order to clear up the water.

But the situation is not hopeless. Relaxation is something that happens by itself—just as water clears as soon as the wind stops blowing. The only thing you can control is your willingness to give this natural process a chance by being quiet and doing nothing.

This might sound simple, but it certainly is not easy. We always have so much to do and the world constantly stimulates us to be busy. So the first thing you need to do is to take the time. Promise yourself to consciously set aside a certain amount of time in which you do not have to do anything. You just allow yourself *to be*.

Your urge to do something will not automatically disappear when you have nothing to do. Memories and plans drag you away from being present here and now. Before you know it, you are thinking about all the things that you have to do.

Paying attention to what is here in this moment is the only thing that can help you to stop. Your breathing—or with the body scan, your body—can become your anchor. It allows you to drift a bit, but always leads you back to being present here and now. At times this means that you will have to bring your wandering attention back again, and again, and again. Here and now is the only place where you can rest. Do it with a smile. It is natural to get distracted. Be kind to yourself. If you get irritated with yourself you only make it harder. And if you do feel irritation, be kind to it. Whatever happens, return to that place where you can be kind with yourself.

If you can pay attention to your body and, in that moment, allow yourself to be free from all other activities, you will see that your body relaxes. Not immediately. At first, you probably become more aware of the tension in your body. You might even get the impression that the tension is actually getting worse. The process of relaxation has its own rhythm. When you give your body and mind the chance, the built up of tension slowly ebbs away.

Finally—you cannot relax if you deny your tension. This can work for a little while. But it is like children who do not get attention. They will keep asking for it until they get it. The same is true for tension. It is important to set aside time for doing nothing. You need that time to come to rest. It is also important to make time to look at the tension itself. Alongside its nurturing effect of attention and relaxation, the body scan can also make us more aware of what is going on in our body, so we can respond to its needs.

“DON'T TAKE IT ALL TOO SERIOUSLY — IT'S JUST YOUR LIFE.”

— GENPO ROSHI

2

AN OPEN INVITATION TO GET OUT OF THE BOX

GETTING OUT OF THE BOX

"TO CONTROL
A FLOCK OF SHEEP
YOU NEED
A BIG FIELD."

— SHUNRYU SUZUKI

Some problems can only be solved if we dare to get out of the box. What box? Most of the time, we are not aware that there are any. Our spontaneous tendency is to look for solutions within the boundaries we have created in our own mind. Sometimes we need to look beyond those boundaries. But how can you do that when you have no idea that they actually exist? Or even worse: that you have created the box yourself?

We are not talking about the norms and rules that we sometimes agree with and sometimes rebel against. There we always have freedom of choice. What we are talking about here are the invisible patterns and limitations within which we daily function.

Mindfulness training is a continuous invitation to get out of the box. By observing ourselves with an open mind, you begin to see things that you did not see before. Mindfulness will unavoidably unveil some of the previously invisible boundaries and what lies behind them. Simply the instruction to set aside 45 minutes each day to practice confronts many of us with obstacles like: "I don't have the time" or: "I don't have the right to spend so much time paying attention to myself." Through mindfulness training you may discover your hidden gentleness or strength. Meditation can confront you with pain that you have avoided for a long time, or with joy that you did not notice before. Mindfulness implies a constant determination to look at what arises. As you see new possibilities, you also receive a natural invitation to respond differently.

This is a never-ending process. That moment when you see it all from every angle just does not exist. The invitation to open and broaden your view is an ongoing invitation. By cultivating mindfulness, we continually keep surprising ourselves.

ATTENDING TO EXPERIENCE

How are you feeling right now? Put this book down for a moment and feel how you are. Do not judge right away. Feel with kind and open attention.

As the training proceeds we will address — during formal exercises (like the body scan) as well as the shorter and informal practices — the things we experience in the course of the day. The idea is to stop and pay attention to moments that usually pass you by. It is a way to learn things about yourself that you often did not notice before.

Let's have a closer look at something pleasant. Choose something small. You may have the impression that you are not experiencing anything pleasant at all. But if you look carefully, you will see that there are always some small things to be found. Especially when things go wrong, it is very useful to develop an eye for these pleasant experiences. Feelings are bodily, they have a physical component. Notice in as much detail as you can what you feel in your body when you pay attention to something pleasant. Discover for yourself which moods, feelings and thoughts are coupled with the experience. Look at how you react to the experience in the moment itself and how you react to it afterwards. Do the same for unpleasant experiences.

In these exercises it is not as important to come up with the right words as it is to give open attention and to learn from that experience. It is about continually learning how we deal with our experiences and how we can respond them with kind attention.

It is like a piece of paper with two smileys drawn on it: one is laughing and the other is sad. Sometimes we are one and sometimes we are the other. They are not neutral. We welcome being happy more than being sad. When we are down we usually try to become happy again as quickly as possible. This is of course natural.

At times we think that it is normal to be happy and abnormal to be sad, or vice versa. Or we say that one of the two is who we really are and the other is the exception. "OK, I may be down in the dumps now but it will not last long. I am a happy person after all."

What would happen if you stopped identifying yourself with one or the other? What if, just for an instance, you would identify yourself with a piece of paper: a white surface that absorbs ink and has room for both smileys and much more. Sometimes excited, sometimes down, sometimes angry, sometimes happy, sometimes.... There is more than enough space. Actually, the space is infinite, or at least as big as your own life. There is room for everything.

Would you now be able to sit and breathe and be the space where it is all happening? Your feelings, your thoughts, your physical sensations, the sounds, the play of the light... without identifying with any one thing. Without saying that one of these things is more you than another.

SIMPLE SITTING INSTRUCTION

Sit in a position that is comfortable, open, and dignified. You can keep your eyes open or you close them. Put your hands on your knees or in your lap.

Do not shut yourself off. Do not wander away but stay present and alert.

Become aware of your breathing. Feel how you breathe in and out.

Whenever you notice that your attention wanders or that you have gotten carried away by your thoughts or feelings, come back to your breathing.

Sitting, breathing, see what comes up. Do not judge. If there are pleasant feelings do not try to hold on to them. If there are unpleasant feelings do not try to push them away.

Stay present, sitting, breathing, with open, kind attention.

Do nothing. Expect nothing. Let it be.

After the meditation has ended see if you can maintain some of this open attention and if you can return to it at moments throughout your day.

MEDITATION IS NOT WHAT YOU THINK

The word meditation is a rather poorly chosen word. If you were to ask twenty different people to define meditation, you would probably get twenty different definitions. None of these definitions would be wrong. The word is just too vague. On the other hand, if you looked up the word "meditation" in Sanskrit, you would not find a word for it. They say the Eskimos do not have one word for snow. They have twenty different words for the white stuff they live in day in, day out. Just as Sanskrit has twenty different words to describe the various activities that we call meditation today.

The original meaning of the Latin word *meditari* is reflection, preparation. It is also used in this sense in the Christian tradition. When the first missionaries travelled to Japan in the 16th century, they saw Zen monks sitting in silence. Their practice made a big impression on them. They automatically thought that the monks were meditating, reflecting on religious matters. When they asked the monks what they were thinking about during their practice, the answers they got were funny, a bit evasive even, like: "Oh, nothing important...."

It took a few centuries before Westerners really tried to understand what it was the monks were doing. We now call it mindfulness training. That is why, when we use the word "meditation" in this book, the only meaning it has is "mindfulness training", the practicing or the cultivation of mindfulness.

Two common misunderstandings need to be addressed here right away. First of all, during meditation you stay in the real world. You are not meant that to float away or go into some sort of trance. This training is called "living in the maelstrom" and not "floating in the cosmos." Mindfulness invites us, time and again, to be present in the here and now, in this moment, and never to escape from it.

Secondly, meditation does not mean you have to stop thinking. If you are attentively present in this moment, you will notice that there are thoughts. Maybe you would prefer those thoughts were not there, but in mindfulness training we let them be just as they are. By shifting your attention, for instance to your breathing, a thought will move into the background, but a few seconds later it may capture your attention again. And that is OK.

Meditation is not what you think. It has different levels of meaning. Do not worry about it. It is only in practicing meditation that its meaning will naturally reveal itself.

WHAT IS KINDNESS?

Kindness is what most of us feel when we see a child trying to take their first steps. You look with a mixture of tenderness and encouragement as they straighten themselves up, try to balance, totter, enjoy the first taste of success, then fall down again and then straighten up again....

When a child falls down, you do not feel angry, nor do you force them back on their feet. You let them find their own way. This is how we learn. When children enthusiastically stretch out their little arms to you, you give them your hands to hold on to and enjoy as they reach their goal.

Most of us do not treat ourselves the same way. We often get caught up in blaming and judging ourselves. As hard as it is, we still beat ourselves over the head when our life is not working out well. We cannot learn this way. We only make it worse.

How can you be kind to yourself? What does it mean to be kind to yourself? You would not accept it if someone else judged you and blamed you in the same way that you do. Hopefully you have enough self-respect to realize that you do not really need to be humiliated and blamed. Why accept from yourself what you would not accept from another?

What is kindness then? The best way to understand kindness is to look at your own yearnings. How would you want someone to treat you when the going is rough? Do you yearn for blame or understanding? For respect or for humiliation? Do you want someone who listens or someone who tells you that you are doing it all wrong (as if you did not know that already)?

Kindness is a conscious decision. It makes no difference why you choose it. Maybe you know that all the blame is counterproductive and only makes it worse. Maybe you do not understand it at all but just want to give it a chance.

Whatever the case may be, kindness is a conscious choice. You choose for it to stop the destructive pattern of blaming yourself. What do you notice then? First of all, you see how deep the pattern of self-blame is. You see that it just does not work. You automatically judge and blame yourself and you cannot stop it. Moreover, you you tend to judge yourself again for this failure.

It is at this point that you need to remember that you can choose to be kind. To judge yourself for not being kind is only more of the same. What can you do? Just as you look with kindness at the child that falls and stands up again, you can look at yourself with kindness. You can look with kindness at the deep patterns that you cannot stop, at your pain, at what you are yearning for. This does not change the pattern—at least not right away. The thoughts stay the same. But handling the situation in this way is actually a radical change.

Have you ever had the feeling that you live in a world without kindness, without love? The answer is simple. Right now, with kind, open attention, you can invite kindness for yourself and for what you find around you. It is in your hands. Now.

I admit
it wasn't the plan
to sleep
during the body scan.

But then that voice
so tender.
I had no choice
but to surrender.

APOLOGY TO FERRIS URBANOWSKI

3

CAN YOU FREELY CHOOSE HOW TO DEAL WITH YOUR LIMITS?

(SELF) RESPECT

During a conversation between the Dalai Lama and a group of Western psychologists and neuroscientists, one of the psychologists noted many people suffer from low self-esteem. The Westerners were surprised that this was a totally strange concept for the Dalai Lama. He could not understand the fact that all Westerners, to one degree or another, were engaged in a constant inner dialogue of self-criticism and self-degradation. The Tibetans who were present during the conversation had no words for it either—literally. The term "low self-esteem" cannot be translated into Tibetan. Thus, the surprise was on both sides. The Westerners discovered that low self-esteem was specific to their own culture.

A nonjudgmental attitude, respect, and kindness are essential to mindfulness. Whatever comes up in meditation is treated with respect and kindness. It makes no difference at all whether these things are your own or someone else's, whether you experience them as inside yourself or outside.

This makes sense in theory. Not many people would protest against respect and kindness as a basic attitude. When we practice meditation it is often not so obvious. If you constantly judge your shortcomings and imperfections, it is not so simple to look at them with respect and kindness. If you usually hide your own weaknesses and not so nice sides it can be hard to look at them with kindness and self-respect.

If you notice that sometimes you find it very hard to be kind, there is only one thing left to do—look at it mindfully, with kindness and respect.

"THIS BEING HUMAN
IS A GUESTHOUSE.
EVERY MORNING
A NEW ARRIVAL.
EVEN IF THEY'RE A
CROWD OF SORROWS,
STILL TREAT EVERY
GUEST WITH RESPECT."

RUMI

DOING AND BEING

We can function in two very different ways: by "doing" and by "being." Usually doing is what we are most used to. Doing is to strive towards a goal. We work for something. And so we are constantly comparing where we are with where we want to get. We measure how far we are away from our goal. You can say that in the doing mode there is a constant feeling of "not there yet." When we do get there, either the doing mode ceases, or we set a new goal for ourselves. Without the doing mode we would not get anywhere. However, a problem arises when we use the doing mode to face something that cannot be at that given moment. When we set a goal that is impossible to be reached. For example, we cannot do anything to change the weather. This is obvious. But there are many things that we cannot fix right away. Feelings, thoughts, and moods come and go following laws that escape our control most of the time. Desperately fighting them in the doing mode will only result in continuous frustration.

The being mode is too often neglected. It is the state of just being without wanting to reach something, without making demands on reality. It is to simply be present. Life is not worth living when we only do and make no room to be. In mindfulness training we consciously cultivate the being mode. Being is simple but not easy. We are so used to *do* that it is hard to let just *be.*

Mindfulness training gives us endless opportunities to practice. Again and again you face the tendency to do. You want to relax, yet you feel more tense. You want to pay attention, yet you wander off. You want to stay awake, yet you fall asleep. You want to breathe calmly, yet your breathing only feels more chaotic. Looking at this from the doing mode you see only failure. If you approach it from the being mode then this is just the way it is. In the doing mode it is contradictory to try to do nothing. Just by trying you are already doing. The same is true for your thinking. Some people think that you learn how *not* to think in meditation, but it is nonsense to try to stop thinking. Just try not to think about a pink elephant. Too late! In the being mode there is not contradiction at all. All the thoughts, feelings, impressions just come and go. They are part of what there is now.

The step from doing to being happens very quickly. By definition you cannot work to get there. You just do it now. You feel like you cannot do it, that you do not understand it at all... and you just let that feeling be there. It is what there is now. Ten seconds later you begin worrying again. OK. Notice it and let it be. Just be.

LIMITS

Stretch your hand up in the air and try to touch the ceiling. Somehow your body knows that you cannot do it, that there is a limit, a boundary. We have our limits and it is not always so easy for us to deal with them.

How do you feel your limits? Some people have a really hard time feeling where their limits lie. Limits are not black and white. There is a wide spectrum. Have you reached your limit when you drop dead, get wounded, are in terrible pain, feel uncomfortable? Pain and tiredness are the signals our bodies give us. Some people feel their limits only when they are in pain or exhausted. Then comes the day when you are sitting at the doctor's without any idea what has happened to you. To make matters worse, you hear that there is nothing wrong with you.

You learn about the whole range of your limits by being with your body with kind open attention. It is like the gas meter in your car. Some drivers always know exactly how much gas there is left in the tank and fill it up when it needs to be filled. Others need to see the red lamp burning and have to rush to the gas station. Others find themselves in a car that suddenly stops....

How do you handle your own limits? Feeling your limits is one thing, knowing how to handle them is another. Is a limit something you automatically see as something to exceed? There is certainly nothing wrong with pushing your limits once in a while, but you need to know them very well and act wisely. A top athlete has to be very careful with the limits of his body when he trains. Otherwise he will overtrain, which will not only have a negative impact on his condition but also lead to injuries.

Maybe you do not want to feel your limits at all. Maybe you only stop when you are finished with what you had planned. Or with what someone else had planned for you. Or when you have done at least as much as everybody else. It is dangerous to put your boundaries outside of yourself. No one else can feel your limits for you.

Through mindfulness training you learn about your own automatic behavior regarding limits. It is not so much about whether or not you go over your limits but whether or not you are conscious of what you are doing. Are you the one in the driver's seat? Are you making the decisions? Are you free to choose how you handle your limits or are you being carried away by all sorts of expectations and automatic behavior?

THE TRAP OF FATIGUE

Pain and fatigue are the body's ways of signaling that we have gone beyond our limit. There are times when our limit is closer than we would like it to be. With certain physical illnesses we have passed our limit even before we have done anything.

The diagrams below can be used to show the onset and the continuation of pain and fatigue. (The words pain and fatigue are interchangeable in the diagram). The diagrams are not applicable to everyone but some of us will certainly recognize ourselves.

The first diagram shows how we can get into trouble. When it all begins to get to be a bit too much for us, the first thing we do is we cut back. We slow down. But what are the things we cancel first? Usually we cut back on the activities that relax and nourish us. It might save us time, but soon the fatigue only increases. This is what creates the trap that ends in exhaustion.

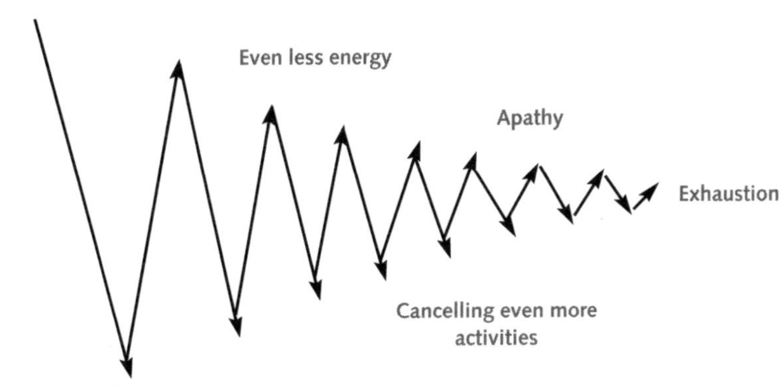

It is essential to care for yourself. You owe it to yourselves as well as to those who need you to care for them. This is not about time and it is not about discipline. It is about priorities.

The following diagram shows how we can get stuck in fatigue (pain). At one point you go beyond your limit even when it seems like you are not doing much at all, and the next minute you collapse. It is a vicious cycle of going from one extreme to the other.

The only way to break out of this cycle and begin to build up your strength is to become acutely aware of your limits and how you handle them.

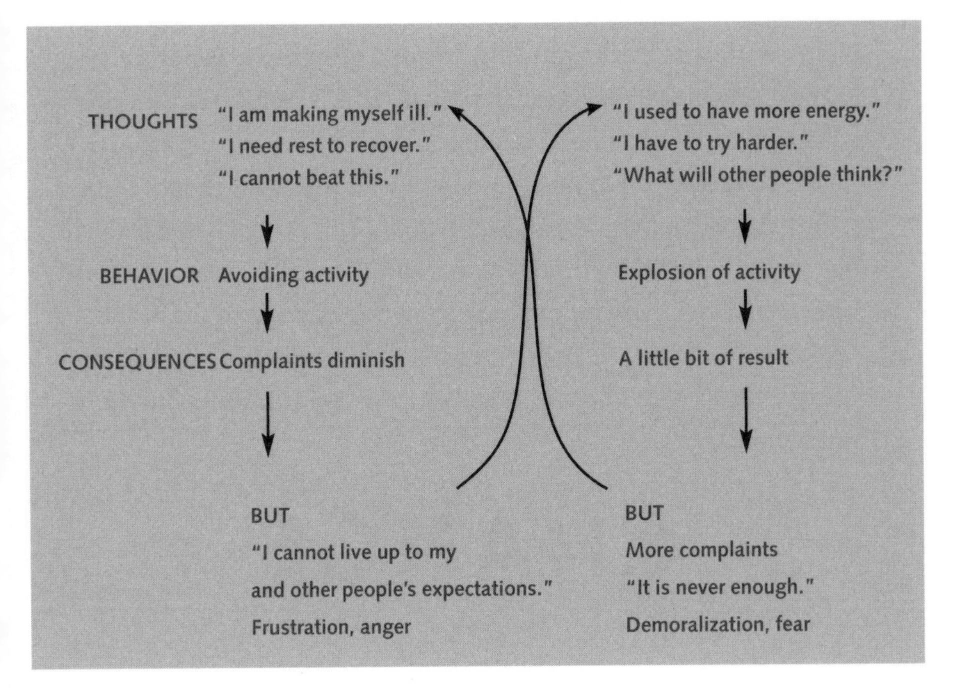
THOUGHTS
"I am making myself ill."
"I need rest to recover."
"I cannot beat this."
BEHAVIOR
Avoiding activity
CONSEQUENCES
Complaints diminish
BUT
"I cannot live up to my
and other people's expectations."
Frustration, anger
"I used to have more energy."
"I have to try harder."
"What will other people think?"
Explosion of activity
A little bit of result
BUT
More complaints
"It is never enough."
Demoralization, fear

CHANGE

Can I still change? Is it too late for me? I get to hear this question a lot—from people in their seventies, thirties, or even from teenagers.

Am I too old to change? Change is inescapable. Getting older is a change in itself. I dare you not to change in the next five years. The crucial question is not *if* we will change, but *how* we will change.

It is tempting to set goals. It is in fashion now: goals, targets, achievable gains. We often do this without considering how to reach our target. A wiser way to change is to point in a direction and not to a goal. A slight change in course now can make a big difference in the future.

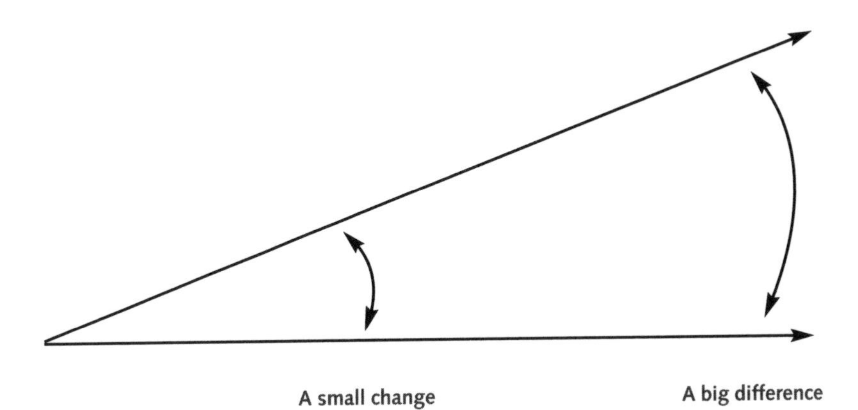

Changing course, even minimally, requires insight. Insight in the course you are following now and its possible consequences, as well as insight in the new course you want to follow and its consequences.

No one has ever learned how to walk without falling and standing up again. Therefore we need to constantly be aware of the course we choose to follow and bring ourselves back to it. Again and again, step for step. This doesn't need to be hard. Just don't make your goals unrealistic, and calmly follow the course you have chosen.

Building mindfulness into your life doesn't seem to bring any spectacular immediate change. What will the result be if you look at what is happening inside yourself and around you with just a little bit more open and kind attention, again and again?

NOW THAT I KNOW THE ANSWERS OF LIFE, THEY CHANGED THE QUESTIONS.

"Much of life can never be explained but only witnessed."

Rachel Naomi Remen

冨嶽三十六景 神奈川沖浪裏
4

PRACTICING WITH WHAT IS THERE

CONTROL

There are many things that are not within our control. This is true not only for those things outside of ourselves, such as the weather or taxes. In mindfulness meditation we notice (maybe to our disappointment) that even such intimate things as our bodily sensations, thoughts, and feelings, are beyond our control. We cannot even control whether we remain mindful or get distracted.

However, mindfulness also shows us where we do have control at a given moment. As soon as we notice that our attention has wandered, we can bring it back again. We can choose to do this gently. When we notice that we push away some experiences and try to hold on to others, we can choose to keep our attention open in the face of whatever we see. (And then we are distracted again and pay attention again and then distracted and then....)

A sure prescription for failure is to fight against what you cannot control. Yet on the other hand, you can turn yourself into a defenseless victim by underestimating your possibilities. In meditation you learn to better see what you can and cannot control.

You can create more freedom for yourself in what you do. You can choose what you do in situations where you usually act on impulse. All of our impulses, old patterns, and emotional reactions don't disappear overnight. They usually stay the way they are, yet you can learn how to deal with them rather then let them automatically deal with you. This way you get to the point where you see that some patterns soften bit by bit.

MAY I HAVE
THE COURAGE
TO CHANGE
WHAT I CAN
THE SERENITY
TO ACCEPT
WHAT I CANNOT
CHANGE,
AND THE
WISDOM TO
KNOW THE
DIFFERENCE.

KINDNESS, RESPECT, DIGNITY

O CROWN OF LIGHT, O DARKENED ONE,
I NEVER THOUGHT WE'D MEET.
YOU KISS MY LIPS, AND THEN IT'S DONE:
I'M BACK ON BOOGIE STREET.
Leonard Cohen

The biggest misunderstanding about meditation is that it is a state of thought-free, peaceful calm. Anybody who has tried to follow their breathing for a few moments knows that it does not work that way.

There are of course moments of calm and relaxation, joy, maybe even ecstasy (why not?) in mindfulness training, but like everything else these moments are fleeting. Meditation quickly brings you back with both feet on the ground. Back into that daily life with its reality, at times beautiful, at times raw. It is like Leonard Cohen sings in "Back on Boogie Street." This is the reality that mindfulness training is there for.

That is why mindfulness training implicitly includes kindness, respect, and dignity. Without kindness, mindfulness can be cruel. As long as your experiences are pleasant it is not so hard to remain mindful. But what happens when they feel unpleasant? You need lots and lots of kindness and respect to stay with your own restless spirit, your sadness, your shortcomings, all of the things that you wish weren't there.

That is also why it is important to sit in a position that expresses your dignity. This way you discover that you can go through rough times without losing your dignity. You learn that your dignity is unwavering, even when you fall flat on your face.

STOP, LOOK, ACT

Meditation has three aspects: stopping, looking, acting. If you ride through a city on the express train you won't see much of the city. First of all you have to stop. But stopping is not enough. If you want to see the city you will have to get off the train and look around. After you have stopped and looked, you can decide what you want to do.

The distinction between stopping, looking, and acting is somewhat artificial. It makes it easier to talk about them, but in reality each aspect includes all of the others. You cannot look at something without stopping, and when you stop you see what is going on.

Attention is the essence of meditation. You need attention to be able to stop, see, and act. And not just attention, but a free, open, kind attention with which you can be present in the here and now.

STOP

We often get carried away by our lives. We run the risk of being lived by all the things that happen, our emotions, impressions, expectations, future, and past. It is very important to stop in order to come back here and now. You can do this by paying attention to something that is present here and now.

One obvious thing we can pay attention to is our breathing. Our breathing is with us in every situation at every moment.

EXERCISE

When you have finished reading this text, put the book down and go to where you are in your breathing. Know if you are breathing in or breathing out. Follow the rise and fall of your breath without changing it. Keep going. Notice how all sorts of thoughts and feelings distract you from paying attention to your breathing. Allow whatever there is to be, and then let it go and bring your attention back to your breathing. Become curious about your breathing. Is it deep or shallow, slow or quick? Be careful not to let yourself get carried away by your anger or frustration at being distracted again and again. Smile at yourself and return again and again to the safe harbor of your breathing.

LOOK

When you regularly practice paying attention to your breathing you will notice moments when you become very peaceful and calm. There will also be moments when you are irritated and restless. Meditation is not only about becoming peaceful. That would turn you into a zombie. Meditation is about stopping and looking at what arises in each moment—including all the restlessness, thoughts, feelings, reactions that are there.

EXERCISE

Return to the previous exercise and pay attention to the rise and fall of your breathing without changing it. Let everything else go. Keep going until you notice that you become distracted. How do you react when you notice that you are distracted? Pay attention to that feeling or thought without trying to change it, just like you did with your breathing. Don't think about it. Don't judge it either. There is no right or wrong way. Just follow it with your attention.

ACT

Looking is not enough. Acting follows looking. As long as something stays self-evident, our reactions to it will be semi-reflexive. Meditation takes the obvious away from the reaction and demands an answer to the situation. Meditation brings attention to our actions.

EXERCISE

Choose something that you do without having to think about it. Maybe this is grabbing a piece of candy, or switching on your TV, or scratching where you itch. Try to become conscious of the impulse to act. Instead of reacting on that impulse, first look at it. Investigate it. What is pulling you? What does it feel like to postpone the impulse? Does the impulse go away or does it get stronger? Now do what you wanted to do, but with attention rather than automatically. What are you doing? What movements do you make? What happens then? Do you like doing it this way or not?

STOP

Stopping is often the hardest moment in mindfulness training. Once we are on the mat or on the cushion, the rest follows, but it can be hard to get ourselves to sit or to lie down. We get so carried away by the maelstrom of our lives! If you wait until you get around to it or postpone things until there is enough time, you will never get started at all.

When we are caught up in the pressure of the maelstrom, reality looks very different. It seems like everything that needs to happen must happen right now. There is certainly no time to rest. It seems like we are indispensable, as if the world would stop if we didn't keep it turning.

Stopping is a conscious decision. Sure you have a lot to do, but right now you make the choice to stop *doing* in order to make room for *being*. This is a whole other perspective on reality. Maybe your restlessness is the first thing that becomes apparent. Maybe after a while you begin to wonder what all the fuss was about. Maybe the time will come when you find stopping beneficial.

Formal practice is not the only thing that is important. Stopping is not limited to 45 minutes an hour (more or less) each day. Stopping is something you do any moment. You do something and you stop. You do something and you stop. The rhythm is natural.

It might be useful to build into your day moments when you consciously stop amid the pressure of your activities. One way to do this is to take a three minute break for breathing. It doesn't even have to be three minutes. Just paying attention to three breaths is a way to stop. Walking meditation is an ideal way to call a halt. You can do this at home, at work, on the street, wherever you are.

You can choose some signals to remind you to stop. There are computer programs that give you a signal when you have been working for an hour on end. Stop, follow your breathing for a few moments and then continue with your work. You can turn every sounding of a bell into a signal. You can let the telephone ring three times, stay with your breathing, and then answer it. You can taste attentively the first bite of each meal. In short, you can think of your own ways to build in moments to stop during the maelstrom of your life.

LIKE GENTLE RAIN
ON MY FACE,
THE SOUND OF THE BELL
COOLS MY HEART.

LOOK

The simplest mindfulness instruction can be summarized in one question: How is now? It makes no difference if you are sitting, standing, or walking. "How is now" urges you to be present with what there is now, with kind, open attention. It is a supremely short instruction that only lasts for an instant. Then you ask it again: How is now?

If you can remember this simple instruction, all the piles of meditation literature, trainings, and courses are superfluous. Body scan, limits, breathing space: this is it in a nutshell.

Maybe this sounds a bit disrespectful, but in comparison to the question "How is now," all other meditation instructions only provide you with something to play with and give you the illusion that you are doing something, so that you will not get too bored and will keep going.

The advantage of an instruction like "How is now" is that you don't need anything else. It is pure mindfulness. The disadvantage is that you don't have anything to hold on to. It is harder to keep on going, especially at the beginning. It seems so senseless, so aimless. And in a way, it is. So how will this question help you? Just wait to be surprised by the effect it will have on you.

This is why we usually start with following our breathing. Breathing is an anchor that you can come back to again and again. You always have it with you. You cannot leave it behind on your night table in the morning. The advantage of the breathing is that it is constantly in motion. You can hold on to it, but not too tightly. This keeps your attention open.

What happens when you look? Well, look....

I CHERISH THIS MOMENT

LIKE A NEWBORN CHILD

I CHERISH THIS MOMENT

LIKE A DYING FRIEND

ACT

Imagine you are driving on the highway when all of a sudden a car overtakes you and cuts in, so that you have to brake and almost get hit by the car behind you. What goes on inside you then? Most people will feel something in their body, in their chest, something building up. Adrenaline, anger....

This is an unavoidable reaction, simply because you have a body.

The question is: What do you do next? In blind rage you could step on the gas, overtake the car, make the driver stop, get out of your car, grab a weapon, and kill the driver. This is not an exaggerated example: there are people in jail for doing this. They usually regret what they have done. An automatic impulse can take you to a place where you do not want to be at all.

There is something else you can do. You can add mindfulness to the situation. This way you will notice that a reaction is building up in your body. You can notice your tendency to react blindly. It's possible in such a situation to respond adequately instead of being determined by the circumstances. Maybe you will choose just to drop it and just let the other car go. After all, you won't get home any later. And maybe once you are home you will tell the story to a family member in a shaking voice.

To react is to act on impulse. Someone says something ugly and you automatically say something ugly back. Or you withdraw into yourself and let them walk all over you, just as automatically.

To respond assumes enough mindfulness for you to notice what is happening and be free to make a choice.

HOW DO YOU LEARN THIS?

Stop, look, and act can be applied throughout your daily life. A while ago, someone responsible for the safety at a nuclear reactor told me that he used the STAR principle. STAR stands for: Stop, Think, Act, Review. He immediately understood what mindfulness is all about.

Where do you learn this? How do you practice stop, look, and act?

The best place is on your cushion or your mat. It is where you learn to stop and to look. Even more important—you learn to stay with it and not run away. You practice with everything that happens to you. All the feelings and thoughts that comes up during meditation are not distractions but opportunities to learn. If you are suddenly overcome with anger or sadness while you are practicing, then stop, look, and don't let yourself get carried away. You learn how to see more and more and you expand your freedom to choose. You learn to stay with the things that you used to run away from. You learn to take distance from what previously would have made you react impulsively. You learn to remain standing where before you would have been knocked over. You learn to remain alert in situations when previously you would have collapsed and let yourself be waltzed over.

This is why mindfulness training can sometimes be more useful (though not easier) when the going gets rough, when you feel tense, anxious, sad, or angry. During the safe space of your practice you learn to stay present with kind, open attention, not to close your eyes, not to run away. You can compare it to the firing range where a policeman learns to use his weapon, or to the simulator that helps a pilot learn what he has to do when the plane's engine catches fire. It is not important how the policeman gets through the firing range. What is important is what he does and does not do when he is in a life-threatening situation. He should not have to take out the manual on how to use his gun at that crucial moment....

On your cushion you practice with what comes up. This raises your chances of responding adequately to the challenges in your daily life. It is a never-ending learning process. The challenge never stops.

BREATHING SPACE

Regularly making time for three minutes of breathing is the exercise that lies between formal and informal practice. It helps those who do not live in a Zen monastery to stop and look in the midst of their busy daily lives.

There are different ways to do this exercise. One way is to ask yourself three questions:

1 HOW AM I DOING NOW?

Stop and ask yourself how you are doing. Get in touch with yourself. Listen, feel, and look at how it is going. Do it with a kind, open attention and without judgment.

2 HOW AM I BREATHING NOW?

Just let everything be as it is, and pay attention to your breathing. Each time you notice that you are distracted, bring your attention back to your breathing.

3 HOW DOES MY BODY FEEL NOW?

Let your attention expand from your breathing to include the sensations in your body. Whatever it is that you are feeling, just let it be and be attentively present with it as you breathe.

Meditation is very simple. It's just sitting and paying attention to what there is. Whatever you hear is what you hear, whatever you feel is what you feel, whatever you think is what you think. Whatever is there is there. Do not push anything away.

You cannot learn it and you cannot get better at it. Whatever is there can change in an instant. Learning and experience are irrelevant.
There can be no teachers or masters. No one is an authority on what is here and now.

5

A CONTINUOUS PROCESS OF HEALING

SELF-HEALING

They say that time heals all wounds. You do need time for healing, but it is not time itself that heals. For time to heal it needs certain qualities. These qualities are attention, space, and mindfulness.

Meditation certainly confronts you with time. Forty-five minutes, thirty minutes, five minutes—it can fly by or seem like it goes on forever. Meditation is preeminently the time for attention and space. You can experience pleasant or unpleasant feelings, be restless or calm, happy or sad, ecstatic or dull, excited or bored, clear or confused, hopeful or in despair.

Meditation makes space for everything. It is becoming space itself. There is not one feeling that is automatically connected to meditation. Meditation is letting everything be without judgment. It is breathing attentively and being present with what is here now.

Meditation goes against our tendency to hold on to what is pleasant and push away what is unpleasant. This is why you need discipline. After you have persevered for a while with this discipline, you will notice a remarkable healing process taking place. It not only touches the deep wounds in our lives, such as loss and grief, but also all the things that cross our path. It is only by having this experience that we can develop a deep trust in the ongoing process of self-healing.

Meditation has its own built-in safety system. We create a safe space by being quiet, by remaining present as we breathe. Without feeling any pressure, we can invite emotions to this space and experience them without feeling threatened or overwhelmed.

However, there is a trap to this experience. Meditation is being present with open attention, without judgment, without expectations. Once you notice that this can be healing, you may start to meditate expecting it to help. This expectation makes it impossible to meditate with open attention. What you have to do then is notice your expectation with open and kind attention, and let it be there.

"HEALING GRADUALLY
TAKES PLACE
WHEN YOU'RE ALONE
WITH NATURE."

J. KRISHNAMURTI

THOUGHTS

At times we are our thoughts, at times we have thoughts, and sometimes our thoughts take charge of us.

Mindfulness training teaches us how to treat our thoughts as events. If you consciously sit and carefully observe, you will see how thoughts come and go. Our head does what it is made to do: generate all sorts and sizes of thoughts.

Some thoughts make sense, others are nonsense. Some are pleasant, others are painful. Some thoughts are correct while others are blatantly scandalous and shameful. (Happily no one can read our minds!) Some thoughts seem to fit us well, while with others seem foreign and we have no idea how they got into our head.

Sometimes the mechanisms that produce a thought are clear. Some of the connections are logical and others are purely associative; sometimes there are old patterns that keep generating the same kind of thoughts.

Some thoughts are heavily loaded emotionally, while others are neutral. The thoughts with the heaviest emotional load usually push themselves into the foreground, so that at times they may seem to be the most "true" or "real."

We have little control over the origin of thoughts. What we call "thinking" is a process of selection. The enormous and sometimes random production of thoughts is what makes us creative. The trick is to select the thoughts which we want to pursue further. This is what we have to contribute.

You can compare it to playing chess or cards. Different moves are possible. Some moves are clearly useless. Others are obvious but perhaps not so wise. It is your move now....

Through mindfulness training you become acquainted with this play of thoughts. You learn to see thoughts for what they are: thoughts. You learn not to be automatically determined by thoughts that come up very strongly. The difference between reacting and responding applies to thoughts as well. Mindfulness training is a process of emancipation. It leads to greater freedom.

HARDNESS

How “hard” are your thoughts? In themselves thoughts are harmless. Some thoughts are very useful and helpful, while others are purely senseless.

Thoughts become dangerous only when you let them harden. “I have been treated unjustly” or “It is my own fault” are thoughts. Mindfulness keeps thoughts fluid. You notice that they are there, the emotional color they have, how they affect your body. This is how you remain free to choose how you will respond to them. You can examine your thoughts and see how relevant they are. You can do something with them or you can drop them.

It is when thoughts solidify and harden that they become problematic. You quickly see the difference when you begin to pay attention. A thought is no longer a thought, but becomes a stifling certainty. You get trapped. The injustice, the guilt, or whatever it is, suddenly becomes an absolute and tormenting fact. You lose your freedom. The apparent certainty strengthens your feelings and before you know it you are sucked into a spiral of thoughts and feelings. The heavier the emotional weight of a thought, the easier it solidifies. Delusions are often “solidified emotions.” If you act on that thought, you only make it worse.

It is only when you are able to stop and look that you see what you are doing. Mindfulness is like the flame of a candle. The solidified candle wax melts again when you put it into the fluid wax. Just noticing what you are doing and looking at it with kind attention is all you need. This requires courage, because most of the time the emotions that are linked to the thoughts pull us in the opposite direction.

This is why meditation is most fruitful—and most difficult—when things are not going well. Again and again you observe how your mind solidifies your thoughts and how they melt when you hold them in the warmth of mindfulness. Again and again. It is a painful and difficult process. But it is enormously liberating.

HAPPINESS

A deep-rooted misunderstanding is that we will be happy when we have everything we want. If only we could win the lottery. If only we could work harder and earn more money. And we fight for it all at the expense of everyone and everything ....

Again and again we see that up until now having what we want has not made us really happy. How long are you happy when you get what you want? How long is it before you start wanting something else?

When you look back, you see that life with all its changes is an unchanging flow of happy and sad moments, some of which are very happy and some unbearably sad. It is not hard to predict that these ups and downs will continue and that all of us will experience happiness and sadness.

Does happiness always slip through our fingers? Is it an unattainable illusion? It depends on how you look at it. Maybe happiness does not have anything to do with getting what you want. Maybe it has something to do with how you respond to the waves of pleasure and pain that come and go.

Maybe happiness is the ability to be glad with the glad things and sad with the sad things.

In the ebb and flow of happiness and sadness we experience many beautiful things. Can you enjoy that? Can you see it? Can you take pleasure in the realization that all is temporary and will pass? Can you enjoy it without trying to hold on longer than is possible?

Can you let the sad moments in without panicking, without despairing at the inevitability of it all? Can you remember that this too will pass?

Can you ride the waves of happiness and sadness without the illusion that they will last forever? "The Bodhisattva joyfully rides the waves of birth and death" is how the meditation teacher Thich Nhat Hanh puts it. One thing is guaranteed: by letting go of the desperation that makes you hold on to the pleasant and push away the unpleasant, you will spare yourself and others a lot of problems. It is never too late to learn how to surf.

"THE BODHISATTVA
JOYFULLY RIDES
THE WAVES OF BIRTH
AND DEATH."

THICH NHAT HANH

MINDFULNESS, INSIDE OR OUTSIDE?

In mindfulness training you pay attention to what is here now. It does not make much difference if you experience something as inside or outside of yourself. It is about the experience as it presents itself. You regard everything as events which are occurring right now. Thoughts, sounds, memories, feelings, physical sensations, images... Absolutely anything can arise during meditation and has a right to be there.

Take a moment to think about the following: you cannot tell the difference between the sound of a tree falling in the woods and the registration of that sound in your head. What you hear is sound. The distinction between the subject and the object of observation is a construction that is later added to the observation. During meditation you just let that construction be what it is—an event like anything else.

There is certainly nothing wrong with constructions. The ability to be able to distinguish between inside and outside, between yourself and someone else, is vitally important. But we haphazardly place limitations on reality that direct and restrict our observations. These are the boundaries we remain within without realizing that they are there. By choosing openness, we make room for new things that are beyond the boundaries.

This means that if you are accustomed to focus mostly on yourself, you are going to notice more things that happen outside of yourself. If you are focused outside of yourself, you will discover more what goes on inside. If you are constantly fixed on certain thoughts or physicals sensations, you will begin to notice that there is more than that.

Mindfulness meditation, therefore, is not by definition an "inner path." For those faced more to the inside, it is a path to the outside, and vice versa. This is one of the nice things about meditation: it makes the world wider and full of surprises.

"ZEN IS STUDYING
THE MIND, STUDYING
THE MIND IS DROPPING
THE MIND;
DROPPING THE MIND
IS BECOMING INTIMATE
WITH ALL THINGS."

DOGEN ZENJI

THREE
THOUSAND
BEES BUZZING
IN MY HEAD.
I LET THE SUN
OF AWARENESS
SHINE
TO SET THEM
FREE.

6

TO CREATE
A SPACE OF
KIND, OPEN
ATTENTION…

LISTENING

Meditation is being attentively present to whatever arises in the here and now without judgment. The formal practices, like sitting meditation, are a simplification of reality. They are exercises in attention. We notice the effects by how attentively we live outside of the formal exercise time.

If we are talking with someone, it is their presence which is arising in the here and now. Listening is the same as meditating. You could even say that formal meditation is a good exercise in listening.

Here, it is also all about stopping, looking, and acting. To listen, you need to stop. If you are busy doing something else it is hard to listen. But stopping is not enough. Listening involves going to the other with our attention. It is letting in the presence and the words of the other without immediately judging or interpreting them. If you get lost in your own automatic reactions, interpretations, and conclusions, then you are no longer openly attentive.

Listening also means having open attention for your own feelings and reactions. There are always two perspectives in communication—how you see reality and how the other sees it. So it is not about what reality is, but rather how you see and experience it. If one of the two perspectives is absent, you really cannot speak of communication. Listening is not losing yourself in the other's story. If you do that, you yourself are not there anymore. During a conversation you might have feelings that are pleasant or unpleasant, restful or restless, happy or sad, ecstatic or neutral, clear or confused, hopeful or despairing. Listening is making room for all of that. This is what gives dialogue its healing power. Just as time heals when there is attention and space, so attention and space given by someone else becomes a healing presence.

AND THUS

A CONVERSATION

UNFOLDED LIKE

A BLOSSOM UNFOLDING

ON A COLD BRANCH

IN WINTER...

HANDLING STRONG EMOTIONS

Emotions can touch us in every fiber of our body. We cannot do anything to avoid this. We do not want the feeling but it is there. It is possible that strong emotions make us do things that we would never have approved of afterwards when things are quieter.

SOLVING IT

When the emotion originates in a definable problem, then it is important to solve that problem. Not every problem can be solved immediately (for example, a serious illness).

Some cannot be solved at all (the death of a loved one). Some solutions are just superficial and do not restore peace of mind (like taking revenge or getting even). The emotion can still linger even after all the steps towards a solution have been taken, and sometimes even after the problem has been solved.

DISTRACTION

When we are overcome by emotion it can be helpful to turn our attention to something else. Doing something pleasurable, such as listening to music, reading a book....

There are also ways of distracting our attention that are problematic: alcohol, binge eating, drug use.... A lot of behavioral problems are very effective ways to turn our attention away from strong emotions, but are extremely destructive in the long run.

An exercise such as the body scan, or focusing on your breathing, can soften the emotion. Finding the courage to sit or lie down and get in touch, deep inside your guts, with your own strength and immovability can be very healing.

But this method is not always successful. There will be times when relaxation and other forms of distraction just will not have the effect we would hope.

MAKING SPACE

What you can do then, is to make the emotion an object of your meditation. This way you create space for the emotion. When you try to close the emotion in a small space you begin to feel like you are going to explode. The powder that launches fireworks just sizzles away once you take it out of its holder. The message here is to create more space.

To begin with, you create space for all the thoughts associated with the emotion. There is a huge difference between 'He's left me in the lurch" and "There's a thought: 'He's left me in the lurch.'" In the first instance you identify with the thought, in the second you have created some room to play. Make sure that the space you create is one of openness and kindness. Turn your attention into a big bowl which has room for your thoughts.

Shunryu Suzuki once said: "The best way to control a flock of sheep is to put them into a big field."

When you do this regularly you may discover patterns in your thoughts. During the meditation. Just let the thoughts come. It may turn out that a thought is an old familiar one. For example: "There's that thought again: 'He's left me in the lurch.'" Once you are able to less identify with your thoughts and give them more latitude, you can let them be what they are (thoughts) and turn your attention specifically to the physical feeling that accompanies the emotion. Every emotion is a physical feeling. It is no coincidence that we use the word "feeling" for feeling. Turn your attention into a big bowl for all the physical sensations that stream through your body. Be vigilant with the same openness and kindness. Be present with boundless kindness for the pain in your body. Breathe along with the stream of sensations in your body.

The goal of this method is not to get rid of the emotion or to lessen it. It is a way to deal with it skillfully. Emotions inevitably end by themselves some point. Neither the deepest misery nor the highest ecstasy lasts forever.
Then what is the effectiveness of dealing with emotions this way?

By not (unwillingly) feeding your emotion you do not keep it going.

You learn to know your emotions and reaction patterns better and to recognize them more quickly.
You create more freedom from your emotion so that you are less susceptible to being taken over by it.
Gradually you increase your resilience.
You create more kindness in your life.

THE FOUR QUADRANTS

If you make a diagram of the ideas in the previous chapter, you get four quadrants. Every strategy for handling difficult emotions has a place within these for quadrants. You can distract your mind from the difficult emotion and fixate on something else or you can create a space of kind, open attention for the painful feeling. You can do this either alone or with someone else.

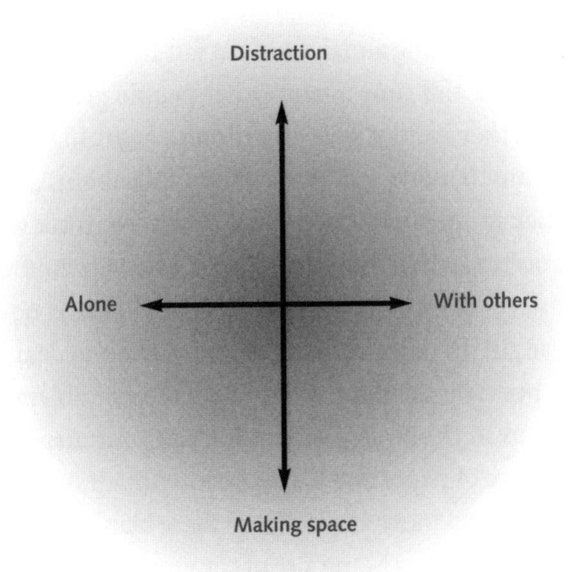

Imagine that you are very sad. You could distract your mind by playing cheerful music (distraction alone). You could also play sad music to make room for the feeling (making space alone). If you turn on the radio you will hear many songs about lost love. There is certainly a market for this. John Lee Hooker sings, "The blues is a healer." You can share your sadness with someone else and cry it out (making space with others). Of course you should do this with someone who know how to listen and who gives you their kind, open attention. You could also find someone to talk to about everything except your sadness (distraction with others). That may be useful too.

There is not one of the four quadrants that is better or worse than the other three. As you become freer in moving through the quadrants, you experience more comfort in handling the unavoidable pain of being alive.

Problems arise when you get stuck in just one of the quadrants. Some people spend their whole lives running away from their feelings. This is exhausting and doomed to fail since our feelings catch up with us time and time again. Other people get so lost in their feelings that they cannot give attention to anything else. There is only one thing that they can think about, talk about.... Addicts often get stuck in the distraction quadrant. They drink when something sad occurs, when they are irritated or angry. And when they win the lottery that sure is a reason to drink. There is nothing else. They get caught up in a vicious cycle: they drink to deal with their problems, but their drinking causes even more problems.

Take a look at the strategies you have at your disposal. Draw a cross on a piece of paper and fill in the four quadrants for yourself. How freely can you move around? Are there blank spaces? Can you think of ways to make a better use of the emptier quadrants?

BREATHING SPACE IN DIFFICULT MOMENTS

Even when you are having a hard time (or better: *precisely* when you are having a hard time!), it's helpful to regularly make space for three minutes of breathing.

The instructions that follow are specifically meant for the times that you are overcome by strong emotions or plagued by difficult thoughts. In both situations you ask the same three questions:

1 HOW ARE YOU DOING RIGHT NOW?

Notice how you are feeling, observe the thoughts going through your head. Name your feelings and thoughts. You can say something like this to yourself: this is the feeling of sadness; this is a judgmental thought.

2 HOW IS YOUR BREATHING RIGHT NOW?

Let everything be as it is and bring your attention on your breathing. Every time you notice that you get distracted just bring your attention back to your breathing.

3 WHAT IS GOING ON IN YOUR BODY RIGHT NOW?

Widen your attention to include what you are feeling in your body. Breathe like you were breathing in your feeling. Do so with a kind, open attentiveness. As you breathe out say to yourself: it's OK; whatever there is, I can take it. Make space inside yourself for all these sensations, no matter how difficult they are.

BAD DAYS

You are having a bad day. Your mood is black. The things that usually interest you now leave you cold. The things you thought you could do well do not work out. What you thought would be bearable is now unbearable. The people who you thought loved you seem to hate you, or at least they are ignoring you. You cannot find rest in anything. Nothing can cheer you up.

You would obviously rather not have days like that, but they happen and sometimes they last much longer than you would like. If only they would just last for one day. At times it seems like they will never end.

What do you do with days like this? I'll summarize it in four points.

1 KINDNESS

We often make it harder on ourselves than it already is by judging ourselves. We hit ourselves over the head because it is happening again. Why? All of that blaming yourself does not get you one step further.

Kindness is the only reasonable alternative. It is important that you at least know what is going on. Kindness is a conscious choice. If you start turning against yourself again, try not to take it so seriously. Maybe you can find a place in yourself where you can look gently at all that aggression (because that is what it is).

2 MINDFULNESS

See what is going on. Notice the thoughts that bring you down. Look compassionately at the dark feelings. Don't turn away but don't make it worse by fighting them. Don't get sucked into them either. Don't cultivate them. Realize that you are not your thoughts and your feelings, that they happen, that they come and go like everything else.

3 THE FOUR QUADRANTS

What can you do to resist your thoughts? How can you make room for what there is? Who could you have a good talk with? With whom can you do something nice?

4 DON'T WAIT

Life is now. We have the tendency at times to think that life begins once the problems are solved. When you wait for the future, the future waits. Don't give up. Live now and do what is sensible and possible at this moment even if it is only something small.

...
Here is your wine
And your drunken fall;
And here is your love.
Your love for it all.

Here is your sickness.
Your bed and your pan;
And here is your love
For the woman, the man.

May everyone live,
And may everyone die.
Hello, my love,
And, my love, Goodbye.

Leonard Cohen
"Here it is"
from *Ten New Songs*

LEONARD COHEN

HERE IT IS

7

GETTING COMFORTABLE WITH NOT KNOWING

MAGIC

There are two kinds of magic. The first is the magic of the stage magician who distracts our attention with his wand, while with his other hand he conceals the egg in his pocket. This is the magic of advertising, of the beautiful men and women, the happy families eating tomato soup, the spotless white wash. This is also the magic of temptation, of stealthy glances and suggestive gestures.

This kind of magic is based on concealment, hiding, and distraction.

There is another kind of magic. The magic of the rising sun, the silence in a forest in the evening, the wind on the beach that almost blows you over. This is the magic of clear contact between two people, of being touched by the expression on someone's face, being moved by vulnerable people, being present, sharing in joy and sadness.

All of this involves the willingness, the courage, and the kindness to see reality as it is now.

Mindfulness training is choosing again and again to be completely honest with yourself. This includes the courage and the kindness to look at yourself as you are without concealing anything. This means looking at what you are feeling right now, looking at what is going on with you right now.

It is possible that at first you will notice how you keep fooling yourself. How you protect yourself against the pain of life by making others better or worse, bigger or smaller. Having the courage to see all the subtle (and not so subtle) ways we fool ourselves is the gateway to the magic of kindness, freedom, and openness.

WE GO FOR MAGIC,
NOTHING LESS.
MAGIC IS NOT SOME
QUACK HOCUS POCUS;
MAGIC IS THAT DEEP
INNER FEELING OF LOVE,
PRESENCE, AND
OPENNESS TO THE
WONDER OF WHAT
IS NOW.

INTIMACY

"MR. DUFFY LIVED
AT A LITTLE DISTANCE
OF HIS BODY."

JAMES JOYCE

The meditation taught in mindfulness training never takes you away from reality. Time and time again you bring your attention back to what is real right now, without adding anything, without illusions, without making it nicer than it is.

This brings us into intimate contact with reality. Unlike Mr. Duffy, we don't live at a little distance from our body. We really feel what is going on in our body right now. We stop running away from it. We become our body again.

If you have become accustomed to living a little removed from your body, this new intimacy may initially cause some anxiety. The body is not just an object. By avoiding our body we often avoid painful sensations, memories, and anxieties.

This is not a problem. These impressions and feelings receive their needed attention again in our recovered intimacy with reality. As always, constant kindness is required. Forcing or overriding resistance are unhelpful. There is nothing wrong with resistance. Resistance is like the brakes of a car. The brakes make the car a safe vehicle. Resistance is part of reality just like any other feeling. Mindfulness brings you into intimate contact with your own resistance. That is fine. This intimacy also reaches the reality outside of ourselves — the sounds, the songs of the birds, the whoosh of the cars racing by, the colors, the play of light and shadow, the people around you.

Being intimate with reality does not mean that you are the victim of reality. The exact opposite is true. Mindfulness helps you to become more intimate with your own "yes" and "no". Within this intimacy lies the freedom to respond and not just to react.

NOT KNOWING

Everyone knows how it feels not to know anything anymore. Most of the time this is a very unpleasant experience. Strangely enough, in mindfulness training we cultivate that feeling.

If I have heard the weather forecast five times during the day I am not going to listen to it a sixth time. By then I know that it is going to keep raining. Mindfulness is kind, open attention. You only pay attention when you don't know.

Not knowing can make us feel very uncomfortable. But then there really is so much that we don't know. What is my life going to look like next year? Tomorrow? This evening? Even though we have an idea what is going to happen, we really cannot be sure. All of us know that our life can change in a split second.

Through mindfulness training we grow accustomed to not knowing. Follow your breathing: you don't know when your attention will wander again. Listen to the sounds: you cannot know what the next sound will be. Look at your thoughts: How can you know what your next thought will be?

Surprisingly enough, as we get used to this feeling of not knowing, it brings us unimaginable comfort.

GRASPING

In the being mode you can let black and white, pleasant and unpleasant, beautiful and ugly just be. The doing mode stops that instantly. In the doing mode we try to form the world according to our own expectations. There is nothing per se wrong with that. But when we become desperate, tormenting ourselves to get what we want and hold on to it tightly, we become the victims of our own desperation. The worst that can happen to our wishes is that they come true. Often our wishes are so limited that they reduce the creativity of life to something very narrow-minded. The world we can control is okay, but true wonder is to be found in the world that escapes our control.

Sometimes we are rudely confronted with things we cannot control. A serious illness, the death of a loved one... so many things happen to us unexpectedly, without our wanting them. Paradoxically, I have often heard people say, "This illness is the best thing that ever happened to me." A serious illness such as cancer puts everything in a new light. It breaks our routine and strangely enough people sometimes experience this as enrichment. It is of course a shame that they had to get ill first. Hopefully we can control the world enough for doctors to discover effective treatments.

Mindfulness training keeps you open to the unexpected even without calamities in your life. You don't have to wait until everything slips away from you to stop and look, look, look.

ANXIETY

When you sit with kind, open attention, anything can come up, even anxiety. A man shared the following dream: "I turned around and saw a woman in a black coat. She had no face. I only saw a dark emptiness. I felt an indescribable anxiety. I ran away." This same man also said that everything he had done in his life had been driven by anxiety.

Mindfulness training means that you stop running away. You turn around and look anxiety right in the face.

In his autobiography Jacques-Yves Cousteau recounts how he and his companions started deep-sea diving. Once they carried out an experiment that involved exploding old grenades underwater. They wanted to test how close they could get to the explosion without being blown up. They were surprised how close they could get while staying out of harm's way. All they felt were the shock waves of the explosion pass through their bodies. This is because our bodies are largely made up of water. The body is composed of the same substance as the shock wave.

Our minds and our anxiety are composed of the same substance in just the same way. We run away from our anxiety. Some of us spend our lives running from our anxiety only for it to catch up with us time and time again. What would happen if you stopped running and looked your anxiety in the face? If you let the shock wave of the anxiety flow through your body? Zen teacher Catherine Pagès tells us, "Let yourself be permeated by the present moment without fear." Look at the anxiety fearlessly. It seems like a contradiction. It requires courage. Breathe and let it come in. You should not force it. Cousteau did not swim right up to the grenade in the first stage of his experiment. Each time he swam closer and closer to find out how close he could get.

Experiment for yourself. By practicing you will discover the hidden secret of mindfulness training.

"LET YOURSELF BE PERMEATED BY THE PRESENT MOMENT WITHOUT FEAR."

CATHERINE PAGÈS

MORE ABOUT ANXIETY

Traveling through Indonesia. The only way to get to that idyllic beach is with a crowded minibus through mountainous terrain. The official sign on the minibus reads: Maximum 7 Persons. But the driver refuses to leave until there are eight of us. After what seems like an eternity the bus eventually leaves with ten passengers. The driver takes off like a madman. The little bus climbs steep inclines and weaves around sharp curves. I see a deep ravine out of the window. Is my backpack with everything I own still on the roof? I am the only Westerner. Everyone else is casually chatting and laughing. It is totally irresponsible. What if something happens to me? None of my family or friends know that I am sitting here on this bus. I cannot ask the bus to stop and leave me out here in the middle of nowhere. When we cross the highest point the driver suddenly halts in a small village. Without a word he gets out and calmly smokes a cigarette with some friends. Completely relaxed. Fifteen minutes later he gets on again and we begin the hellish descent....

Sitting in meditation with our anxiety is one thing. Anxiety in a situation of real or imminent danger is another. If you are on a boat in a storm your anxiety doesn't get much comfort from the oars, the anchor, or the mooring ropes. It is in situations like this that your mindfulness training can be unexpectedly put to the test. Don't think that you can meditate your anxiety away. Anxiety is a totally normal feeling. It is supposed to be there. When you are in danger it is not the time to start sitting or trying to relax. Can you keep breathing? Can you be anxious and let the storm flow through you? While every muscle in your body is tense, can you adequately handle the situation?

What happens if you utterly fail? Can you fail and still be kind?

"MANKIND OWNS
FOUR THINGS
THAT ARE NO GOOD
AT SEA —
RUDDER, ANCHOR,
OARS, AND THE FEAR
OF GOING DOWN."

ANTONIO MACHADO

HOMESICK FOR REALITY

Her son is the same age as mine. They were born a few days apart. They are both one year old. She is wearing a kerchief on her head as she looks at me. She doesn't like wigs. Her husband is with her. He treats her with care and devotion. All three of us realize that her prognosis is bad.

It is the first meeting of our meditation course. She asks me why someone chooses a profession like this. She can understand why someone becomes an oncologist but why choose to work with the pain, the sorrow, the despair that people suffer?

I am often asked this question. Why do I choose to do this? I keep coming up with the same answer. It is not so easy to put it into words. I have started calling it "homesick for reality".

When I first began working as a psychiatrist and psychotherapist I was faced with a huge question: How will I be able to handle all this suffering? Clearly, closing the door behind me or drowning everything away with alcohol were not practical solutions. Hiding my emotions behind a professional façade was not something I wanted to do or could do.

The only solution left was to face reality and live with the ever present realization that people suffer. To live with that knowledge that it in the past I had so hard tried to avoid. My own meditation practice became sitting with that realization, my work centered around not pushing that suffering away.

It has given me more than I could ever have hoped for. Not bitterness, but rather an intimacy that carries in it a reality that is more beautiful, more intense and satisfying than I ever imagined: a realization of being welcome in this reality, even when it involves illness, suffering, and death.

I look into the eyes of my own son. I realize his vulnerability. I don't know what life has in store for him. I enjoy his presence. Now.

The blue hills are of themselves blue hills;

The white clouds are of themselves white clouds.

The wild geese do not intend to cast their reflection;

The water has no mind to receive their image.

Nothing whatever is hidden;

From of old, all is clear as daylight.

8

THE EIGHTH WEEK LASTS THE REST OF YOUR LIFE

CONNECTED-NESS

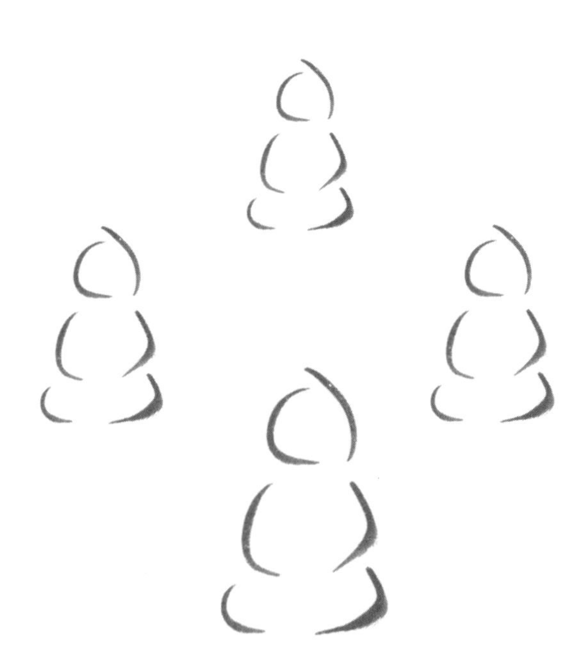

Meditation is something you always do alone. Even when you sit together with people in a group, you sit alone.

Yet meditation is something you never do alone. Even when you sit meditating by yourself, you are connected with all the generations of people who have gone before you, with the people who are meditating now, with every being that can feel, suffer, enjoy....

IS THIS BUDDHISM?

Mindfulness originates in the Buddhist tradition. Mindfulness is the word for *sati*, which is one of the elements of the Buddhist eightfold path. Thich Nhat Hanh, the Vietnamese Zen teacher, has given mindfulness a central place in his teaching. One of his first books, *The Miracle of Mindfulness*, is a compilation of letters written to volunteers who were trying to help at the height of the Vietnam War. The letters were written to support them during the almost unbearable stress of the war.

So we can call mindfulness an authentic Buddhist practice. The biggest difference with the Buddhist practice is its limits. The boundaries of mindfulness training are clear.

1 THE MOTIVATION

You practice mindfulness training to improve your personal situation. People train because they want to cope with stress in their own lives. That stress might be the result of a life threatening illness, too demanding job, anxiety and depression...

In true Buddhist traditions, you do not only focus on your own personal wellbeing, but also on the well being of the other. However, mindfulness training does not exclude the wellbeing of the other completely, since caring for yourself will in turn be good for the people with whom you come into contact.

2 THE PRACTICES

In mindfulness training we limit ourselves to formal and informal meditation. Other forms of Buddhist practices, such as rituals and moral guidelines, are not part of the training. They are limited to customs that are practiced in hospitals and in health care.

During the training we do not get into the ethical and philosophical aspects of Buddhism. However, the emphasis on being kind to your own experience does echoe the ethical element. The philosophical element is also implicitly present in the whole concept of stress and mindfulness.

3 THE DURATION

One of the advantages of an eight-week training program is that the time is clearly limited. You can manage eight weeks. However, the eighth week lasts the rest of your life. If you are practicing alone, you decide how long and how often you will practice in the future.

The awareness of boundaries gives us freedom of choice. You can respect the boundaries and the safety they offer. And you can choose to cross them. This is always your own choice.

ZEN AND PSYCHO-THERAPY

At first sight it is not really fair to compare Zen with psychotherapy. Western psychotherapy is 100 years old. Freud's *The Interpretation of Dreams* dates from 1900. Zen, on the other hand, is a 2,500-year-old-tradition. The dharma has withstood the test of time while psychotherapy is still developing.

Yet we cannot really write a book on mindfulness and not make the comparison. A lot has been said and written already. Some see Zen as a superior form of psychotherapy, others feel both have nothing in common. Some people, like Ken Wilber, see Zen as a continuation of psychotherapy and say you should undergo therapy before you begin Zen.

I can only add my own personal opinion to this controversy. I approach it from three angles:

1 THE DHARMA AND PSYCHOTHERAPY

Masao Abe reported on the meeting between C.G. Jung, one of the founders of Western psychotherapy, and Sinichi Hisamatus, a prominent Zen teacher. Jung contented that his method dissolves complex after complex. Hisamatsu remarked in amazement that this cycle will never end and proposed that the dharma deals directly with the root of suffering. Jung was surprised and did not understand how that was possible.

This dialogue points to the crucial distinction between Zen and psychotherapy. Psychotherapy solves personal problems (it doesn't make any difference if you formulate these problems in internal psychic terms or in terms of behavior). Zen is not interested in problems, but focuses on suffering and attempts to put an end to all suffering. Not only to your own personal suffering, but to the suffering of "all living beings" as is recited in the Bodhisattva vow.

This means that Zen and psychotherapy each have their own distinct role and right to exist. Psychotherapy will never lead to liberation or enlightenment. It is an illusion to think that Zen will solve your problems.

It is fine to be detached from your car but it does not solve the problem of a flat tire. Without the tools or the capacity to repair the flat tire, you will need the help of a passer-by. The same is true for all the personal problems you cannot solve yourself. You need help from a passer-by, a psychotherapist. If you practice Zen, then it is important that you find a therapist whose value system is not in conflict with the compassion and wisdom (karuna and prajna) Zen strives for. This is not so easy since many psychotherapeutic schools maintain ego-centered value systems.

2 MEDITATION AND PSYCHOTHERAPY

Meditation is a technique that you can use within the context of the dharma as well as outside of it. If I look at myself, I realize that nothing has changed me more than meditation. Since both meditation and psychotherapy bring about change, we are again faced with the question about the relationship between the two. Most comparisons of meditation and psychotherapy miss the point that both are a way of formalizing two different elements which continuously arise in daily life. Meditation formalizes attention and psychotherapy formalizes dialogue.

Psychotherapy is a special relationship of formal contact with an outsider during which a dialogue develops in an attempt to formulate a problem. (Varying therapeutic contexts use different ways to formulate but the global structure remains the same.)

Meditation is a very special way to come to a halt in your life and to look at what is happening in the moment.

Yet psychotherapy is not possible without attention, and meditation is not possible without dialogue. People are constantly changing and both attention and dialogue help that change along, though in very different ways. Through dialogue the process of change is guided, named, given form. Attention brings about spontaneous openness which makes space for change without knowing in advance where that change will lead.

Two people followed a meditation course because they felt so tired.

The first said: "I am just as tired as before but now I can do much more." The other said, independently of the first: "I am just as tired as ever but I do much less and enjoy so much more."

By virtue of their differences, meditation and psychotherapy can be complementary.

3 ZEN AND THE PSYCHOTHERAPIST

I myself began with Zen while completing my training as a psychiatrist. The practice of Zen has changed the therapist. The following outlines how the dharma has influenced my development as a therapist.

Suffering

During my training as a psychiatrist, I was taught to identify abnormalities and disturbances. As soon as I began practicing Zen, I was shocked to discover that meditation is first and foremost about suffering and not disturbances. In my work, I had to deal with tremendous human suffering that asked for understanding and healing. This doesn't mean that the concept of "psychic disturbance" is meaningless, but rather that it is always a secondary tool for understanding suffering. This means that when I meet a patient, I first of all try to understand them as someone who is suffering and seeking a way out of that suffering, no matter how strangely they may behave. That way, a lot of things don't seem so strange any more. Recognition of suffering is the starting point for every therapeutic contact.

Compassion

It follows from the above that the therapeutic attitude is one of compassion. While my training as a psychiatrist emphasized a professional distance, room steadily grew within that professional distance for compassion for the often intense suffering of the one seeking help.

The professional relationship remains—in all of its asymmetry—a relationship between two fellow human beings characterized by compassion. A lot of the human suffering and problems that find their way to the therapist are very often the result of lack of compassion, of the merciless aggression that people inflict on others and on themselves. Psychotherapy places a great emphasis on aggression (physical, sexual, psychic). The alternative is systematically excluded. The patient (literally: the one who suffers) as well as the therapist both often do not realize that compassion is the only reasonable antidote for so much senseless aggression.

Meditation

My experience with meditation has taught me that a spontaneous process of self-healing begins when you create a space of openness and compassion. Emotions soften, confusion gives way to clarity and stubborn habits lose their strength.

So at times I teach people meditation techniques not only for relaxation but also as a support for the spontaneous ability for self-healing that we all have. This also means that I try to see each meeting, however short, as a kind of meditation. What I mean by this is that I see it as a shared open space characterized by compassion where anything that arises has a place, has a right to be there, is OK. This doesn't mean at all that there is more silence. Words give form to a conversation. It's much more about the quality of attention, of presence, just as the quality of attention makes the difference between sitting and sitting.

CONCLUSION

I would like to summarize these three perspectives with three pieces of advice:

1. Don't expect meditation to solve all your problems.
2. If you go into therapy be sure to keep up your meditation practice. It can be really supportive for the therapeutic process.
3. Find a therapist with a warm heart.

SIMPLICITY IS INEXHAUSTIBLE

J. KRISHNAMURTI

The various traditions of meditation often use story telling. The Zen koans are very well known. Koans are short legends which hold a clear message.

In one of the koans the Buddha holds up a flower at the moment he is expected to give a talk. Everyone looks at him with surprise. Only Kassho smiles. The Buddha says: "Here I have the deepest insight and I pass it on to Kassho."

Everyone looks with surprise at the Buddha, wondering what the flower means. What is behind this all? Only Kassho understands that there is no special message, that there is nothing to seek beyond the flower. There is only a flower, without any hidden meaning.

Maybe someday they will make a koan that goes like this: "Jon Kabat-Zinn gave everybody a raisin. The participants looked at him with surprise. Only Peter smiled...."

If you expect too much from mindfulness training you run the risk of constantly searching for a hidden message to satisfy your expectations.

There is none.

Mindfulness is simple: being present in the reality that is there at every moment, without adding anything, without seeking anything behind it. Being present with an endless kindness. It is shocking in its simplicity. Its inexhaustible simplicity. The only sensible response is a smile.

FURTHER READING

Jon Kabat-Zinn, *Full Catastrophe Living: Using the Wisdom of Your Body and Mind to Face Stress, Pain, and Illness* (revised edition), Bantam Press: 2013.

Mark Williams, John Teasdale, Zindel Segal & Jon Kabat-Zinn, *The Mindful Way Through Depression: Freeing Yourself from Chronic Unhappiness*, Guilford Press: 2007.

Thich Nhat Hanh, *Touching Peace: Practicing the Art of Mindful Living*, Parallex Press: 2009.

Suzuki Shunryu, *Zen Mind, Beginner's Mind*, Shambhala: 2011.

Joseph Goldstein & Jack Kornfield, *Seeking the Heart of Wisdom: The Path of Insight Meditation*, Shambhala: 2001.

Pema Chödrön, *When Things Fall Apart: Heart Advice for Difficult Times*, Shambhala: 2000.

IF I CAN GET ALL THAT MY HEART DELIGHTS IN, WHY SHOULD I WANT FOR MORE?

www.lannoo.com

Design: CitroenCitroen and Studio Lannoo
Cover Image: The Great Wave off Kanagawa by Katsushika Hokusai
Illustrations: Philippe de Caluwé
Translation: Hank Malinowski

ISBN 9789401419741